DEEP RIVER PUBLIC LIBRARY

3 6035 00053911 0

W9-BFM-252

Sava

4/14/04
I

# Rally Cars

## By Jeff Savage

**Consultant:**
Sue Robinson
Performance Rally Manager
Sports Car Club of America

DEEP RIVER PUBLIC LIBRARY
150 Main Street
Deep River, CT 06417

Capstone press

Mankato, Minnesota

Capstone High-Interest Books are published by Capstone Press
151 Good Counsel Drive, P.O. Box 669, Mankato, Minnesota 56002.
http://www.capstonepress.com

Copyright © 2004 by Capstone Press. All rights reserved.
No part of this publication may be reproduced in whole or in part, or stored in a retrieval
system, or transmitted in any form or by any means, electronic, mechanical,
photocopying, recording, or otherwise, without written permission of the publisher.
For information regarding permission, write to Capstone Press,
151 Good Counsel Drive, P.O. Box 669, Dept. R, Mankato, Minnesota 56002.
Printed in the United States of America

*Library of Congress Cataloging-in-Publication Data*
Savage, Jeff, 1961–
Rally cars / by Jeff Savage.
    p. cm.—(Wild rides!)
    Includes bibliographical references and index.
    Contents: Rally cars—Early rally races—Designing a rally
car—Rally cars in competition.
    ISBN 0-7368-2431-6 (hardcover)
    1. Automobile rallies—Juvenile literature. 2. Automobiles,
Racing—Juvenile literature. [1. Automobile rallies. 2. Automobiles,
Racing.]  I. Title. II. Series.
    GV1029.2.S28 2004
    629.228—dc22                                                    2003014552

**Editorial Credits**

James Anderson, editor; Kia Adams, series designer; Patrick D. Dentinger,
    book designer; Jo Miller, photo researcher

**Photo Credits**

Corbis/AFP, 6–7; David Reed, 16; Hulton-Deutsch Collection, 10
Getty Images Inc./Bryn Lennon, 14; Clive Mason, 25; Grazia Neri, 18, 20, 21;
    Reporter Images/Grazia Neri, cover
John Rettie, 4, 8, 12, 17, 22, 26
Photo courtesy of John Buffum, 28

The publisher does not endorse products whose logos may appear on objects in
images in this book.

1  2  3  4  5  6  09  08  07  06  05  04

# Table of Contents

# Learn about:

- **Rally car speed**

- **Rally courses**

- **Rally car models**

CHAPTER 1

# Rally Cars

The rally car driver grips the steering wheel and waits for the signal. The codriver holds the route book. The starter counts down from 10 to one, lifts the green flag from the windshield, and shouts, "Go!" The rally car bursts from the starting line.

The rally car speeds along a dirt road at almost 100 miles (160 kilometers) an hour. The codriver gives directions. The driver steers the rally car into a sharp turn. The car skids sideways. Dirt flies into the air. The codriver looks at the route book and warns of a tree ahead. The driver barely avoids the tree. The car bumps over boulders and rattles over an old cattle fence.

The car passes the red checkered flag and crosses the finish line. The driver presses the brake pedal hard to stop. The codriver hands a time card to the finish timers, who record the team's time. One stage of the race is done. Eleven stages remain in the ProRally race.

## Rally Car Races

Rally car races take place on country roads. These roads are usually unpaved. They might be logging trails or mountain roads. Rally cars race one at a time from the starting point to the finish line. Race officials use clocks to record each car's time.

Each race section is called a stage. Rallies usually have 12 stages. Stages are from 3 to 20 miles (5 to 32 kilometers) long.

Rallies are often held over two days. Six stages are run each day. The team that completes all the stages in the least amount of time wins the race.

Drivers travel from stage to stage on paved, public roads. These trips are called transit sections. They can be from 1 to 100 miles (1.6 to 160 kilometers) long. Cars are not timed during transit sections. Rally drivers must obey all traffic laws on transit sections.

Rally cars speed over unpaved roads.

**Rally cars are standard cars with a few changes.**

## Types of Rally Cars

Rally cars begin as standard cars. But they are modified for racing. These cars are street legal. They also must have a roll cage and racing seat belts.

Drivers prefer small sedans made by companies such as Ford, Volkswagen, Subaru, and Mitsubishi. Some popular models are the Ford Focus, Volkswagen GTI, Subaru WRX, and Mitsubishi Evolution.

The cost of a rally car depends on the level of competition. Basic rally cars can cost about $6,000. These cars are purchased used. Top competition cars can cost as much as $250,000.

Professional racing teams may spend $100,000 or more each year to keep a rally car in top condition. Large rally teams, such as Mitsubishi and Subaru, spend millions. Racing teams often replace a car's engine or transmission between races. The teams also buy extra tires, lights, and other items they need for each race.

# Learn about:

- **Press On Regardless**

- **World Rally Championship**

- **RallyCross**

CHAPTER  2

# Early Rally Races

Rally car racing is the world's second most popular racing sport, behind Formula One racing. Rally racing has been popular in Europe, South America, and New Zealand since it began more than 80 years ago.

## The First U.S. Rally Races

The first rally races in the United States were held in Detroit, Michigan, in the 1940s. Stages were set in and around the city. The races took place overnight.

In 1948, the first performance-style rally took place in Michigan. The race was called Press On Regardless. The race became an annual event. Later, it became part of the World Rally Championship (WRC).

**The Rim of the World Rally is part of the ProRally Championship.**

The WRC is the world's most popular series of rally races. This series is held in different countries around the world. The series is sponsored by the International Automobile Federation. Countries that host these races include England, Germany, New Zealand, Turkey, Argentina, Australia, and Spain. The United States last hosted WRC races in the early 1980s.

## New Races

The ProRally Championship started in 1973. ProRally is sponsored by the Sports Car Club of America (SCCA). In the early 1990s, the ESPN network started showing these races on TV.

Rally car racing has grown in recent years. The SCCA also sponsors two lower levels of rally racing, ClubRally and RallyCross. In 1998, 4 percent of SCCA members took part in rallies. By 2003, that number had grown to 12 percent.

# Learn about:

- **Suspension systems**

- **Turbo engines**

- **Antilag system**

CHAPTER **3**

# Designing a Rally Car

Rally cars have become faster in recent years. Suspension, engine size, and tires are some features that affect the speed of a rally car.

## Basic Structure

Aside from the stickers on the car, a rally car looks like a standard car from the outside. One major difference is the suspension system. A rally car's chassis is raised higher than the chassis on a standard car. Durable shocks support the chassis. These changes help the car travel over dips and bumps on the ground.

The inside of a rally car looks much different from a standard car. The carpet and upholstery are removed to help make the car lightweight.

The seats are replaced with racing seats made of plastic and foam. The seats have racing seat belts. The belt goes over both shoulders, then fastens between the legs. Steel pipes are welded into the car to form a roll cage.

A rally car's interior has extra gauges for the driver and codriver.

## Engines

The size of an engine used in rally cars depends on the level of competition. Cars in lower-level rallies, such as RallyCross, often use V-6 engines. These engines have six hollow tubes called cylinders. The cylinders form the shape of a *V*.

Rally cars with turbo engines can travel up to 120 miles (193 kilometers) per hour.

Cars in the WRC series have turbocharged engines. A turbocharger is a series of tubes and pumps connected to an engine. It pumps extra air and fuel into the cylinders. The extra fuel forces pistons in the cylinders to move up and down at a faster rate. The pistons then give the engine more power.

## Transmissions

A car's transmission allows the driver to shift gears to go faster or slower. Rally cars have manual transmissions. The driver uses a shifter to change gears.

When a standard car shifts from one gear to another, there is a pause before the car gains full power. Some top-level rally teams add a machine called an antilag system to the cars. This system takes away the pause between gears. Transmissions with antilag systems can cost up to $30,000.

## Tires

Drivers use strong tires that provide good traction. The driver and codriver have to change a tire that blows out during a race. Race organizers limit the kinds of tires drivers can use. Rally car teams come prepared for each race. They bring different types of tires, depending on the weather.

**Rally teams have a supply of tires for each race.**

**Rally teams use tires that get good traction in snow.**

Some events allow drivers to use snow tires. These tires improve handling in snow and mud. Snow tires have deep treads. The treads dig into the snow, dirt, or mud to create better traction.

# Learn about:

- **Competition levels**

- **Events**

- **John Buffum**

CHAPTER 4

# Rally Cars in Competition

Anyone with a car, a seat belt, a helmet, and a driver's license can compete in a RallyCross event. Codrivers are not required. Hundreds of rally car races are held each year across North America. The SCCA sponsors events for all levels of racing.

## SCCA Racing Levels

Each year the SCCA ProRally Championship includes nine races throughout the United States. Racers are divided into five classes. The classes are grouped by engine size and drivers' experience.

Drivers only compete against drivers with similar cars. The top class is called open class. Cars in this class are four-wheel drive with turbocharged engines.

Other classes are Group 5, Group 2, Production, and Production GT. Racers in these groups usually drive cars with V-6 engines.

The SCCA ClubRally Championship includes 50 races. The SCCA divides ClubRally races into three classes called coefficients.

Coefficient 1 events are the shortest events. The stages for these events cannot total more than 30 miles (48 kilometers). Coefficient 2 events have up to 65 miles (105 kilometers) of stage road. Coefficient 3 events can have up to 100 miles (160 kilometers) of total stage distance.

The SCCA sponsors 120 RallyCross events each year. These races are often held in dirt parking lots or open fields.

## Spectators

Thousands of people watch rally races. They stand or sit in safe areas along the race course called spectator stages. They see drivers steer their cars at top speeds over rough ground.

**Some rally cars are not able to continue after a crash.**

Spectators see plenty of crashes, too. About 40 percent of rally cars do not finish a race. Some cars slide off the road into ditches or creeks. Others crash into trees or boulders. Sometimes car engines stall or start on fire.

**Mud flies up around a rally car as it races on the Rim of the World course.**

## Rally Championships

Some ProRally Championship courses are more difficult than others. The Rim of the World race in Palmdale, California, is known for its dangerous curves over desert sand. The Sno*Drift race in Atlanta, Michigan, is sometimes run over snow. The Pikes Peak International Hillclimb in Colorado Springs, Colorado, rises from 9,000 to 14,000 feet (2,740 to 4,270 meters).

The winner of the SCCA ProRally series each year earns the winner's trophy and money from sponsor companies. Racing teams place a sponsor company's logo on their car or race uniforms. In exchange, the company gives the team money.

Many ProRally drivers and codrivers dream of racing in the World Rally Championship. Carmakers sponsor teams in this series. WRC cars are modified more than SCCA rally cars. The cars have six gears and four-wheel drive. Winners of the WRC are often known as the best rally racers.

# John Buffum

John Buffum is the greatest U.S. rally racer of all time. He holds many rally racing records.

Buffum was born October 4, 1943, in New Haven, Connecticut. He grew up in nearby Wallingford.

In the 1970s, Buffum studied math in college. During that time, he discovered the thrill of rally car racing. He often competed as a codriver.

By 1975, Buffum began driving in rallies. From 1975 to 1988, he won the U.S. National Championship 11 times. By 1987, he had won 119 events worldwide. This number of wins broke the world record. The following year he became a team owner and manager.

# Glossary

**chassis** (CHASS-ee)—the frame on which the body of a vehicle is built

**cylinder** (SIL-uhn-dur)—a hollow chamber inside an engine in which fuel burns to create power

**modify** (MOD-uh-fye)—to change; designers modify the body or engine of a rally car to make it more powerful

**roll cage** (ROHL KAYJ)—a steel pipe that is welded to a rally car to protect the driver and codriver

**suspension system** (suh-SPEN-shuhn SISS-tuhm)—the system of springs and shock absorbers that cushions the up-and-down movement of the chassis

**traction** (TRAK-shuhn)—the grip of a car's tires to the ground

**treads** (TREDS)—bumps and deep grooves on a tire; treads help tires grip surfaces.

**upholstery** (up-HOLE-stree)—the stuffing, springs, cushions, and covering that make up a car's seats

## Read More

**Dubois, Muriel.** *Pro Stock Cars.* Wild Rides! Mankato, Minn.: Capstone Press, 2002.

**Raby, Philip.** *Racing Cars.* The Need for Speed. Minneapolis: Lerner, 1999.

## Useful Addresses

**Canadian Association of Rallysport**
595 Elm Road
Stouffville, ON  L4A 1W9
Canada

**Sports Car Club of America**
P.O. Box 19400
Topeka, KS  66619-0400

**United States Auto Club**
USAC National Office
4910 West 16th Street
Speedway, IN  46224

## Internet Sites

FactHound offers a safe, fun way to find Internet sites related to this book. All of the sites on FactHound have been researched by our staff.

Here's how:

1. Visit *www.facthound.com*
2. Type in this special code **0736824316** for age-appropriate sites. Or enter a search word related to this book for a more general search.
3. Click on the **Fetch It** button.

FactHound will fetch the best sites for you!

## Index